CONNOISSEUR'S LIBRARY

AMERICAN ANTIQUES

JAMES AYRES

WORLD PUBLISHING
TIMES MIRROR
NEW YORK

Contents

Published by The World Publishing Company
First American edition
First printing—1973
Copyright © Istituto Geografico De Agostini, Novara 1973
English edition © Orbis Publishing Limited, London 1973
All rights reserved
ISBN 0-529-05012-9
Library of Congress catalog card number: 72-10446
Phototypeset in England by Petty and Sons Limited, Leeds
Printed in Italy by IGDA, Novara

Designed and produced by Harriet Bridgeman Limited

Library of Congress cataloging in publication data

Ayres, James.
  American antiques.

  (Connoisseur's library)
  Bibliography: p.
  1. Art objects, American. I. Title. II. Series:
Connoisseur's library (New York)
NK805.A94   745.1'0973   72-10446
ISBN 0-529-05012-9

WORLD PUBLISHING
TIMES MIRROR

Acknowledgements
Abby A. Rockefeller Collection, Williamsburg: 87. Art Institute of Chicago, Chicago: 11, 22, 24. Baltimore Museum of Art, Baltimore: 7. Boston Museum of Fine Arts, Boston: 9, 12, 34, 36, 43. British Museum of Natural History, London: 89, 90, 91, 92, 93. B.P.C. Publishing Limited, London: 2, 3, 4, 6, 18, 19, 20, 21, 25, 26, 27, 28, 29, 33, 48, 49, 50, 51, 52, 53, 54, 55, 56, 57, 58, 59, 61, 62, 63, 64, 65, 78, 80, 81, 82, 83, 84, 85, 86, 88, 94, 95, 96, 97, 98, 99, 100, 101, 102, 103, 104, 105, 106, 107, 108, 109, 110, 111, 112, 113. Copyright Reserved: 79. Corning Museum of Glass, Corning: 66, 67, 68, 69, 70, 72, 74, 76, 77. Henry Ford Museum, Old Sturbridge: 32. Henry Francis du Pont Winterthur Museum, Winterthur: 1, 5, 10, 15, 16, 38, 40, 45. Jay Cantor: 23. Metropolitan Museum of Art, New York: 8, 17, 41, 60. Mount Vernon Ladies' Association of the Union, Mount Vernon: 13. New Orleans Museum of Art, New Orleans: 71. Orbis Publishing Limited, London: 30, 31, 44, 46. Sandwich Glass Museum, Sandwich: 73. Sotheby's Belgravia, London: 75. White House Collection, Washington, D.C.: 14. Yale University Art Gallery, New Haven: 35, 37, 39, 42, 47.

Influences on American design

The American flag has thirteen stripes, which symbolize the thirteen original States, and fifty stars, emblematic of the fifty States in the Union today. As an object, the flag derives from the coat of arms of the patrician who became a rebel, George Washington.

From Alaska in the north to Texas in the south, from Hawaii in the west to Maine in the east, air-conditioning has removed the climatic conditions that affected the design of people's homes, and efficient air freight, coupled with deep freeze storage, has given us the luxury of any foods at any season throughout the year. In the past, Man had none of these benefits and as a result he was sensitive to his environment at both practical and aesthetic levels. In northern New England, for example, the old farms consist of a complex of buildings under a continuous umbrella of roofs from the farmhouse to the byre. In the south, a plantation mansion stands aloof and unencumbered by its dependencies, for even the kitchen was removed to a small separate building some distance away.

Material considerations apart, the other great influences upon America were the traditions of her various immigrant groups, the American Indian having been ruthlessly abolished in most areas, except the south west, as a cultural force at an early date.

The systematic colonization of the Americas by Europeans began after 1492. It is thus possible to study, within a relatively compressed time-scale, the manner in which foreign cultures transmuted themselves into ways that are identifiable as American. Black Americans, for example, with limited or no rights and few, if any, possessions have made their contribution almost exclusively to the oral traditions of music and literature.

In the sixteenth and seventeenth centuries and later, the Spanish settled in regions that today form part of the United States, as did the Dutch, the French, the Russians, the Germans and groups from Sweden, Ireland and Scotland. Once Britain had finally gained mastery of the New Netherlands in 1674, British political power and subsequent social and political influence extended broadly from New England almost to Spanish Florida.

In 1607 the first permanent British settlement in North America was established at Jamestown, named in honour of James I; later settlements along the James River formed the province of Virginia in remembrance of Elizabeth I. Virginia was regarded as a land to be exploited just as New England was a region where the persecuted could become the persecutors. To a greater or lesser extent, European Colonial powers saw their colonies in North America as a source of raw materials. In 1743, for example, the British Board of Trade wrote to Governor Wentworth of New Hampshire as follows: 'It is our express Will and Pleasure that you do not upon any Pretence whatever . . . give your consent to a Law or Laws for setting up manufactures . . . which are hurtful or prejudicial to this Kingdom'.

In 1690 the population of the British Colonies in North America is thought to have been about 200,000, compared with an estimated 2,500,000 by 1776. This small population meant that the luxury crafts were often slow to develop, whilst others were pursued at a non-professional cottage industry level, as was the case with weaving. Furthermore, the fashionable 'planters' in the south and merchants in the north tended to prefer items from Europe. Silver was an exception to this rule, as it was the one craft that kept abreast of European fashions and was the least original aspect of Colonial American craftsmanship.

In general, American Industry did not begin to emerge until Independence. In 1793 Eli Whitney (1765–1825) contracted to supply the U.S. Government with 100,000 muskets in two years. American mass-production methods were developing.

Nevertheless the official catalogue of the Great Exhibition of 1851 says of the United States Section: 'There were two causes which gave to the productions of American industry displayed in the Great Exhibition a character totally distinct from that which is found in those of many other countries. In the first place whole districts are solely devoted to the pursuit of agriculture, disregarding mining, trades, and manufactures; and secondly, in the United States, it is rare to find wealth so accumulated as to favour the expenditure of large sums upon articles of luxury'. It was the Civil War that provided the necessary incentive to create the great industrial power which America has become today.

Furniture

It is likely that most of the early settlers in Jamestown and Plymouth Plantation brought with them from England a chest or trunk in which to house their personal belongings.

In America the use of native woods resulted in furniture that was truly original and essentially American. The English furniture forms that inspired American craftsmen had long been discontinued in England though they no doubt persisted in the provinces. This time-lag may be attributed to a recollection of styles which could not take a practical form until a later date. The so-called 'Hadley' chests that were made by the Allis family of Massachusetts and Connecticut are good examples of new materials, coupled with a failing memory, producing a new form.

Chairs were uncommon in America until the second half of the seventeenth century, a fact due in part to the social conventions of the 'Old World' where only the head of the family was the 'chair man'. Three types of chair were in use: the turned or thrown, the wainscot, and the so-called 'farthingale' chair – a type that was frequently covered with turkey-work. Forms and stools were in regular use but it was not until the eighteenth century that chairs could be described as being common articles of furniture.

The restoration of Charles II brought about a considerable improvement in household comfort, much of which was inspired by the surroundings that the exiled monarch had known in France and the Netherlands. William of Orange had as his Minister of Works a Parisian-born Huguenot, Daniel Marot, whose influence upon English design was considerable. It was his designs that formed the basis for a large part of the early eighteenth-century English and British Colonial furniture. American examples of the style employed American walnut, cherry and white cedar in less elaborate forms than English examples, which were embellished with seaweed marquetry and the geometric form of parquetry.

In the late seventeenth century a great variety of woods were used for veneering but eventually walnut found favour above all others. This wood varies greatly in type and the French, Italian, English and American varieties are easily identifiable. During the Queen Anne period, carving was kept to a minimum and shapes were restrained in order to exploit the natural beauty of the grain.

The American furniture industry developed fast and soon became a potential rival to that of Britain. This is reflected in a Government Report of 1732 in which it appears 'that the people of New England, being obliged to apply themselves to Manufactures, more than other of the Plantations, who have the Benefit of a better Soil and warmer Climate, such Improvements have been lately made there in all Sorts of Mechanic Arts, that not only scrutores, Chairs, and other Wooden Manufactures . . . are now exported from thence [as 'venture' cargo] to the other Plantations, which, if not prevented, may be of ill Consequence to the Trade and Manufactures of this Kingdom'.

In the eighteenth century a number of pattern-books were published in England that were to transmit the knowledge of new fashions to British Provinces and Colonies alike. John Vardy's 'Some Designs of Mr. Inigo Jones and Mr. William Kent' (1744) influenced both American archi-

tecture and furniture, and above all Thomas Chippendale (1718–79) with his 'The Gentleman and Cabinet-Maker's Director' (1754, 1755 and 1762) was responsible for publishing the designs of his generation, most notably those of Matthias Lock, so that they were accessible to all.

Just as the *élite* colony of Anglo-Irish who lived in eighteenth-century Ireland evolved an elegant way of life, the background to which was a style of furniture and furnishing today known as Irish Chippendale, so, in a new urban setting, America produced an urbane American who commissioned furniture now known as American Chippendale. The term is usually applied to furniture that was derived from the English, mid-eighteenth-century, post walnut, pre-satinwood epoch and made, as Joseph Downs said, 'in the spirit of the original but new in conception'.

The three basic sources of mahogany were Cuba, San Domingo and Honduras. The finest was the Cuban, a wood that is characterized by great weight, hardness and closeness of grain. When it is worked, minute white flecks of a chalky character appear in the wood. Honduras is lighter

Left: Armchair, New England. Late seventeenth century. (American Museum in Britain, Bath.) Above: Girandole clock by Lemuel Curtis (1790–1851). Early nineteenth century. (Christie, Manson and Woods Ltd., London)

Some of the most remarkable makers of this magnificent furniture were Quakers, such as the Goddards and the Townsends of Newport, Rhode Island, and William Savery of Philadelphia. In the whole history of American Colonial furniture, the Townsends and the Goddards (the two families intermarried) are truly remarkable for the quality of their work and altogether some twenty individuals from three generations made furniture. The combined efforts of the brothers Job and Edmund Townsend produced for Nicholas Anderse in 1767 'a large mahogany desk' at £330, a fee which demonstrates the respect which they commanded in their own day.

Block-front carcase furniture (in which the central panel recedes in a shallow concave between slightly convex panels) seems to have been unique to North America. Some early eighteenth-century English bureaux include certain block-front features but Chippendale did not illustrate any furniture of this type. It is thought that the style originated in the area of Boston, Massachusetts, in the second quarter of the eighteenth century and that it later assumed characteristics of Chippendale's style. The first known documented piece is a fine bureau-bookcase by a Boston cabinet-maker that is signed 'Job Coit 1738'. Job Coit's daughter-in-law married for the second time into the Townsend family of Newport, where many fine block-fronts were made. Sometimes the 'blocking' of drawer-fronts is carved from the solid and this probably accounts for the surrounding cock-bead usually being part of the carcase rather than of the drawer.

In England the chest-on-stand, or 'highboy', of the late seventeenth and early eighteenth centuries was abandoned in favour of the 'tallboy', or chest-on-chest, where the lower section is supported on low bracket feet. In contrast the highboy is supported on high cabriole legs, the top being surmounted by a swan-neck pediment, the centre of the pediment being usually embellished with a cartouche. Chippendale illustrated a few examples of the chest-on-stand which he called the 'chest-on-frame'; the stand or frame is of a very simple type and encloses no drawers within its frieze. In eighteenth-century America the highboy was known as a 'high chest of drawers'. They are usually elaborately carved, as it was customary for such pieces to be put on display in the drawing-room, despite the fact that they were designed to contain belongings of a personal nature. John F. Watson noted in his 'Annals' (1829) that 'every household in that day deemed it essential to his continuance of comfort to have an ample chest of drawers in his parlour or sitting-room in which the linen and the clothes of the family were always of ready access. It was no sin to rummage for them before company. These drawers were sometimes nearly as high as the ceiling'. The lowboy, as its name implies, was in effect the lower part of the highboy. Most of the brass hardware found on American furniture of this period was imported from England, but a few American makers are known.

English provincial 'Chippendale' chairs often exhibit features of Queen Anne or early Georgian character while their construction includes the dowelled 'through-tenons' more favoured at an earlier period, and even the most sophisticated American furniture betrays these provincial characteristics.

In marked contrast, America developed the English

in weight and colour and the mahoganies from San Domingo and Jamaica fall somewhere between Cuban and Honduras in quality. Various patterns in the figuring of that wood were sought after, including 'flame' (from the 'pair of trousers' or crotch of the tree) and the mottled grain of 'plum pudding'. Large quantities of these mahoganies were imported into the United States, although in the American Chippendale period cherry was more often used than mahogany by Connecticut cabinet-makers. Colonial Americans of non-British descent adopted the English language and way of life, and so American furniture in the manner of Chippendale was created by men who were of varied origin. For example, Jonathan Gostelowe who worked in Philadelphia was of Swedish extraction, and Andrew Gautier was a Huguenot.

5

Windsor chair into a highly sophisticated piece of furniture fit for 'Piazza or Gardens', and, in Philadelphia, members of the Continental Congress sat upon Windsor chairs.

The American Windsor usually has stick-backs of hickory and seats of pine, whereas English examples use ash or yew for the backs, and elm for the seats. As a result the American version has a more elegant, elongated back and a thicker seat which it was necessary to chamfer with the result that the legs sprang from nearer the centre. These ingredients produced exaggerated lines. Windsor chairs were usually painted, the most popular colour being green. In America simulated bamboo Windsors were painted yellow and these were popular as early as the late eighteenth century. Various types of Windsor chairs were made including those with 'writing-arms' and the settee version.

In America, as in England, chair-making was a distinct department of furniture-making, its requirements demanding specialist craftsmen to construct an article that had few right-angles, a fact which rendered cramping up difficult. In particular, on curvilinear examples, it was customary to leave projections on the component parts of a chair in order to facilitate the application of cramps when gluing. These projections were subsequently carved off. Another frequently employed method involved the use of a long strip of flexible metal on each end of which a block of wood was bolted; the strip of metal could then be wound round the chair and pulled up with cramps on the blocks. On both sides of the Atlantic there were craftsmen who made both chairs and case-furniture, but they were the exception and it was usual for them to emphasize this fact in their trade cards as did Jonathan Gostelowe of Philadelphia whose card declared him to be a 'Cabinet and Chairmaker in Church Alley'.

Records dating from just before the American War of Independence prove that there were many skilled craftsmen in the country. In Boston, for example, in the English Chippendale period, there were one hundred and fifty known cabinet-makers, chair-makers and carvers, while in Newport there were over fifty. In the south, craftsmen-slaves were able to produce good work. Thomas Elfe of Charleston, whose records for the years 1768 to 1775 have survived, wrote of many 'handicraft slaves', for instance 'five cabinet-makers at £2,250'.

Paradoxically, independence meant a greater dependence upon London fashions, made possible by the publication of an increasing number of British designs by such men as Robert Adam, George Hepplewhite, Thomas Sheraton and Thomas Hope.

The furniture-makers soon followed the lead of Robert Adam, many of whose designs were utterly impracticable for the materials and the scale for which they were intended, so that it became necessary to develop substitutes for carving. But it was the designs of men like Hepplewhite which popularized this style in such publications as 'The Cabinetmakers' and Upholsterers' Guide' (published in 1788, the year that the Federal Constitution was ratified) and Sheraton's 'Cabinet-Maker and Upholsterer's Drawing-Book' (1791–94).

Broadly speaking, early Federal furniture owes much to Hepplewhite and Sheraton while later designs evolved from a synthesis of the work of Thomas Hope and the French Directoire and Empire styles. John Aitken of Philadelphia who made furniture for George Washington may be associated with the earlier phase just as Duncan Phyfe (1768–1854) of New York is the unmistakable leader of the later Federal style. Though traces of French design occur occasionally in the work of Duncan Phyfe, the leading exponent of the French Empire and Directoire styles in New York was Charles-Honoré Lannuier (1779–1819). His work must be considered as French rather than American and it is significant that he did work for Napoleon's brother, Joseph Bonaparte, when in exile in New Jersey.

In England the Queen Anne period may be categorized as the age of walnut and the period that followed as the age of mahogany. The furniture of Hepplewhite and Sheraton was typically constructed in the satinwoods. From about 1800 to 1840, West or East Indian satinwood was sometimes used in America for veneer though a few examples of the use of the timber in the solid are known. However, just as sycamore (renamed harewood when stained) was used in England, in America birch and maple became substitutes for the more expensive woods from the Indies. In the later Federal period brass inlay was occasionally used but it is rarely found on American furniture. Both the Queen Anne and Federal periods demanded simple forms to emphasize the beauty of selected timbers or painted decoration.

More important from a socio-economic standpoint, were the movements towards industrialized methods of mass production. Furniture-making had for a long time been divided into various branches. In England there were the bodgers of High Wycombe and in America there were the Windsor and rush-chair makers of New York. In addition there were other specialists – carvers, gilders, veneer-cutters, turners and upholsterers. These divisions were necessary because of the differing nature of the various crafts but such specialization was also only a step from mass-production methods.

Lambert Hitchcock (1795–1852) was one of the first makers of mass-produced furniture, and his Boston rockers and side-chairs with their stencilled decoration in gold on a simulated rosewood or ebony ground were popular from the 1830s to the 1850s.

Clocks were very rare in Colonial America until a clock-maker, Eli Terry, realized that if he could bring the price of clocks down he would increase the demand for them. In 1792 he opened a shop in Plymouth, Connecticut, in which he manufactured four thousand wooden long-case movements in three years. Mass-production techniques were applied to making cog-wheels of cherry and pinions of laurel, which were mounted upon an oak plate. In mid-eighteenth-century America, high quality clocks had been made by men such as David Rittenhouse of Philadelphia; those made in the nineteenth century, such as shelf, banjo, acorn and girandole clocks of high quality were made by makers like the Willards of Boston. Connecticut and Boston became the leading areas for clock-making and American mass-produced clocks formed an important part of the American exhibit at the Great Exhibition held in London in 1851.

The free forms of some contemporary furniture are made possible by the use of such materials as plastic. In the mid-nineteenth century, papier mâché was used to this end. There was, however, a second method that achieved these results, namely the use of laminated wood. John Henry

Belter refined this method by using the steam-press to create the basic shapes of his designs as seen, for example, in the generous and voluptuous curves of his chair-backs. Born in south Germany in 1804, he emigrated to America in about 1840. Just as Hitchcock was designing in the weakening tradition of a classical revival so Belter's furniture was a fine example of the Victorian rococo revival.

While Hitchcock developed a good breakdown of labour, Belter developed important industrial machinery involving two patents, one of which, dated 23 February, 1858, was for the 'improvement in the method of the manufacture of furniture', entailing two major innovations. The first provided a means of pressing chair-backs into curves on two planes (curve on curve) and the second involved the means by which several such chair-backs could be produced simultaneously.

The Greek, gothic, rococo, renaissance (Elizabethan) and Louis XVI styles all had their revivalists and disciples. As in Europe, nineteenth-century design in America was revivalist, for the Victorians were fickle in their taste though traditionalist in their outlook. Egyptian motifs recurred as a result of an intermittent interest in Egypt caused by the arrival in New York in 1825 of the first major collection of Egyptian art to cross the Atlantic, while Verdi's 'Aida', commissioned to celebrate the opening of the Suez Canal, was first performed in America in 1873.

Alexander Roux began his career in the eighteen thirties with the 'Gothick' and in the 'forties went on to the Italian renaissance (Elizabethan) and rococo styles; by the sixties he was working in the Louis XVI and 'antique' or 'Egyptian'

styles. French names like Badoune, le Prince, Marcotte and Roux dominated New York furniture-making. America did not just look to Europe for aesthetic philosophies, she imported her craftsmen. In the nineteenth century, American furniture lost the originality that had distinguished the earlier work, for the inspiration, the design, the designers and the makers were all adopted. Of course there were exceptions; men like Hitchcock whose methods were new, and religious groups like the Shakers whose work was refreshingly simple. 'All things must be made . . . according to their order and use' and 'all work done, or things made in the church ought to be faithfully and well done, but plain and without superfluity – neither too high nor too low' was how 'Father' Joseph Meacham (1742–96) put it in his book, 'Way Marks'.

Curiously the arts and crafts movement, which was so important in Britain in all aspects of the decorative arts, was far less significant in America although some designers were certainly influenced. One of them, however, spoke in praise of the machine and as a further paradox he was to prove more a prophet of the future than a survival from the past. In 1893 Frank Lloyd Wright established his first architectural practice and in the following year published some 'Propositions' that were virtually a manifesto for his 'oak period' which ended in about 1910. 'Bring out the nature of the materials, let their nature intimately into your scheme. Strip the wood of varnish and let it alone – stain it . . . go to the woods and fields for colour schemes. Use the soft, warm, optimistic tones of earth and autumn leaves'. Wright was working in Chicago and moreover he had been employed in the office of Adler and Sullivan. Although others worked in this idiom, notably Gustav Stickley and Charles and Henry Greene, its period was short lived.

Block-front bureau, possibly made in Boston. c.1770. (American Museum in Britain, Claverton Manor, Bath)

Silver

American silversmiths were not subject to a system of hall-marks, with a brief exception in Baltimore in the early nineteenth century. By and large the position of American silver was similar to that of American pewter, for which personal marks were used, subject to no official control.

Thomas Howard of Jamestown and John Hull (1624–83) are recorded as 'goldsmiths' (self-styled) in the first half of the seventeenth century. Hull was successful in Boston and in 1652 he was appointed Mint Master to the Court of Massachusetts; by permission of the Court he took another English silversmith, Robert Sanderson (1608–93), into partnership with him. These two silversmiths indicate the strong English influence of this very early American silver which was inevitably transmitted to their apprentices who included Jeremie (Jeremiah) Dummer (1645–1718), William Rouse (Ros), Timothy Dwight (born 1654) and, most notably, John Coney (1655–1722). It was this second generation of silversmiths who were to develop their own particular style.

In New York (the New Netherlands) it was the Low Countries that supplied the first settlers and indeed the craftsmen to make their lives more comfortable. Dutch names are therefore common in this region, for example, Peter van Dyke, Bartholomew Schaats, Benjamin Wynkoop, Konraet ten Eyke, Jesse Kip and Cornelius van der Burgh, who was the first native-born New York silversmith.

The Huguenots were prominent in America, as in England, as silk-weavers and silversmiths. Grignon, Soumain and the Le Roux family, as well as Paul Revere (Rivoire), were members of this group who produced essentially European silverware.

The lightness of mid-seventeenth-century silver inevitably gave way to a weighty, more substantial baroque style and this in its turn surrendered, in about 1720, to the elegance of the rococo.

Some of the work of Jacob Hurd (1702–1758) or Joseph Richardson Sr. shows a trend towards American rococo design. The form became somewhat lighter, while the decoration, repoussé, chased or engraved, became more insistent. The Palladian symmetry of man-made perfectionism gave way to rococo asymmetry derived from nature.

The most famous of all American craftsmen was Paul Revere (1734–1818). Though now known chiefly as a patriot, in his own day he was one of the most active silversmiths in Boston and, on the evidence of his surviving day-books, he appears to have undertaken work for other silversmiths such as Nathaniel Hurd (1729–1777), Samuel Minott (1732–1803) and John Coburn (1725–1803). He put his skill as an engraver to use for the cause of Independence. Revere's work, like that of so many other craftsmen, was English in character rather than French, for he was apprenticed to his father Apollos Rivoire, who in turn was trained by John Coney, originally an apprentice to the silversmithing partnership of Howard and Hull who were both English born. After Independence, America needed every skill available and Revere, in addition to his work as a silversmith, dentist and printer, became a bell-founder and copper worker – in 1809 he supplied copper for the boilers for Robert Fulton's steamship.

The Federal style of American silver in which Revere also worked can be seen too in the work of the Richardsons of Philadelphia and John W. Forbes of New York. By 1820 American Empire silver had, at last, achieved a national

Teapot and stand by Paul Revere II (1735–1818). (The Paul Revere Life Insurance Company, Worcester, Massachusetts)

identity. Later, in 1853, 'Harper's Monthly' was able to print 'the time is not far off, we feel sure, when we shall have no need of foreign designers of our plate and jewellery'. Nevertheless, for the next twenty-five years American manufacturers continued to be dependent upon immigrants. Tiffany and Company relied on men like Gustave Herter who had emigrated from Germany in 1848. By the late 1870s a native-born American, Edward C. Moore, working for Tiffany, had gained European recognition. American silver of the Victorian period followed the main trends discernible in the other branches of the applied decorative arts. Art Nouveau was not so dominating a force in American design as it was in European, but in American silver and glass the fashion was adopted with supreme elegance and international acclaim.

Ceramics

Pre-Columbian American Indians made 'hand-built' earthenware vessels, the form and decoration of which was often inspired by the basket-work cooking-vessels that had preceded them.

Bricks were made in Jamestown as early as 1612 and by 1649 'tylemakers' prospered in the settlement. A number of potteries were established and commemorated in place-names such as Potbaker's Corner, Potters Creek, Clay City, Pottertown, Jug Town and even Kaolin. Some North Devon Barnstaple Pottery and Delft and Bristol Delft tiles were imported.

The output of small Colonial potteries producing simple household wares in a coarse red clay was supplemented after Independence with the production of grey stoneware. Redware pottery was usually decorated with white slip which turned to a honey colour on the application of the lead glaze.

A Moravian community established at Wachovia, North Carolina, started a pottery in 1756 with a Brother Gottfried Aust as the master potter making redware, clay pipes and stove-tiles. In 1768, this pottery was moved to Salem, North Carolina, where it continued in production until about 1830. In emulation of Wedgwood, the Moravians also made creamware and many of the German settlements in Pennsylvania produced decorative sgraffiato ware. Another religious sect, the Zoarites, established potteries in Ohio and Indiana in the nineteenth century and marked some of their ironware and black or buff-glazed redware 'Zoar'.

A group of colonists from Staffordshire were active potters at Steeds, North Carolina, between 1740 and 1750 but, in spite of their background, they appear to have produced nothing but the simplest of 'dirt dishes'. In contrast, Andrew Duché (1710–1778), also working in the south, may possibly have made porcelain in addition to earthenware.

Humble potteries were also active in New England, for in 1775 it has been estimated that in the Massachusetts towns of Danvers and Peabody there were seventy-five potters at work.

The Shenandoah Valley became, in the nineteenth century, the centre of a flourishing series of potteries dominated by the Bell Family. Peter Bell was active between 1800 and 1845 and his three sons and five grandsons continued the business at Waynesboro, Pennsylvania, until

1899 and at Strasburg, Virginia, until 1908.

In the latter part of the nineteenth century Cincinnati, Ohio, became the centre of American 'art' pottery and between the years 1879 to 1889 six potteries were operating in that city: T. J. Wheatley, the Cincinnati Art Pottery, the Matt Morgan Art Pottery, Rookwood, Avon Pottery and a sixth pottery that signed its work 'Losanti'. Others, such as the Lonhuda Pottery and Samuel A. Wheeler's commercial pottery at Zanesville, were also active in Ohio at this time. By 1890 only the Rookwood Pottery had survived.

On 25 November, 1880, the first kiln was fired at the new Rookwood Pottery and like other potteries in the district it was probably influenced by the English arts and crafts movement. It was the declared intention that Rookwood should maintain a high artistic standard. Established by Mrs. Maria Longworth Nichols, a prominent member of Cincinnati society, the pottery was named after her father's estate and because its name 'reminded one of Wedgwood'. Old friends of Mrs. Nichols employed by the firm included William Watts Taylor, who became manager in 1883 and owner in 1889. No doubt it was the dilettante element that caused the firm to lose money and Mrs. Newton's father subsidized the enterprise for some years. Its wares were simple, basically Oriental in shape with floral decoration such as the 'Iris' or commemorative subject-matter. Glazes included a rich brown, orange or yellow, though sometimes a smoky blue was used. Autumn colours were popular in the closing years of the nineteenth century.

Rookwood exhibited at the Chicago World Fair where it was hailed as 'an indigenous American art' and at the Exposition Universelle in Paris in 1900. The high standards established by the firm were maintained until about 1920 although it remained in production until 1941. In 1899 Artus van Briggle, who had trained at Rookwood and studied in Paris, opened a studio in Denver, Colorado, producing wares that were consistent with the aesthetics of the Chicago School of Architects of whom Louis Sullivan was the Elder Statesman. Boston was also an important centre for art pottery and, under the Robertsons, the Chelsea Keramic Art Works produced objects inspired by Oriental examples while John G. Lowe's Art Tile Works specialized in decorative architectural features such as fireplaces and dadoes.

Because of the fear of lead poisoning, post-Revolutionary America turned with some enthusiasm to the use of stoneware with its salt glaze which was produced by sprinkling common salt on the vessel before firing. Stoneware is similar to earthenware, but it is fired twice and in a kiln at a temperature of not less than 2,000°F. In America these simple utilitarian wares were made from buff clay and after about 1800 they were often lined with brown Albany slip. They were usually decorated in cobalt blue with free-hand brush-strokes, and many were impressed with names such as 'Woodruff/Cortland', 'Brown Brothers/Huntington L.I.', 'Pea Cross/Hartford' or 'X.P.' for Xerxes Price. Bennington, Vermont, was a popular centre for the manufacture of these wares but, as most of the suitable clays were found in New York State, the main centres of production were there. With the general drift west, such wares were produced in Ohio using the Ohio River clays.

Excavations have proved that imported Chinese porcelain services were used in the elegant houses of Colonial

America on the great plantations of Tidewater, Virginia, and in mercantile centres such as Philadelphia and Boston. English porcelain was seldom used at this time though some examples have been found. The earliest porcelain factory known in America was established in 1770 by Gouse Bonnin and George Morris in Philadelphia and on the evidence of about twenty known pieces their work appears to have been strongly influenced by Worcester porcelain.

After the War of Independence, even more Chinese porcelain was imported although George Washington and John Adams used dinner-services from France. The incumbents of the White House down to Lincoln showed a preference for French porcelain which was uncharacteristic of Americans in general.

The American trade with China followed the usual European pattern and the most typical porcelain imported at this time was decorated in underglaze blue. The patriotic emblems that are sometimes found on imported porcelain would have resulted from designs being sent out to China for a special order.

In 1826 William Ellis Tucker set up a porcelain factory in Philadelphia. This venture was so successful that others followed and by about 1875 the United States of America could boast of an indigenous porcelain industry.

Glass

The first glass factory founded in America was the Jamestown Glass House, established in 1608. It was joined by a second factory in 1621. Only four other glassworks are known to have functioned in America in the seventeenth century, at Salem, Philadelphia and two in New Amsterdam. These factories made window-glass and bottles. At Jamestown glass beads are thought to have been manufactured for trade with the Indians. Window-glass is known to have been made in ten or eleven pre-1776 factories, many of which were in New York.

Eighteenth-century American glass is dominated by three names: Caspar Wistar, Henry William Stiegel and John Frederick Amelung. All three were German immigrants and thus they were working within an essentially European tradition. Some contact was made with English glassworks and it is known that Richard Wistar, the son of Caspar and in 1752 his successor, imported window-glass and hollow-ware from Bristol while Stiegel employed both German and English glassworkers. Wistar's main livelihood, in addition to his brass button factory, came from making window-glass and bottles, but his workers made spare time or 'off-hand' hollow-ware from the dark green and aquamarine glass destined for bottles and window-glass. This 'South Jersey' type of glass is decorated with a form of trailing patterns of molten glass and applied leaf prunts. This tradition of glass-making continued as late as 1860 in regions other than New Jersey.

Henry William Stiegel (1729–1785), though also involved with iron founding, established his first glassworks in 1763 and, with his 'American Flint Glass Works', was the first manufacturer in America to specialize in the production of coloured and colourless flint glassware. Much of this Stiegel glass is decorated with engraving and enamelling, though he also manufactured moulded bottles decorated with a distinctive diamond or hexagonal flower in relief.

Glass of the Stiegel type made by men trained in his factories continued to be manufactured in Ohio until the nineteenth century. Stiegel's success was enormous but prosperity fed extravagance and his death was preceded by bankruptcy.

The brass button maker Wistar and the ironfounder Stiegel were joined by a third man, John Frederick Amelung, who was trained as a glassmaker. All three worked in the Maryland, Pennsylvania, New Jersey region. Amelung's glass is similar in type to that of Stiegel.

Notwithstanding the failure of these eighteenth-century glassworks, there were, at the beginning of the nineteenth century, about twelve glass factories in production; by 1820 there were forty and by 1830 their number had increased to about ninety. Sand for the glass and fuel for the furnaces are two necessities for a glassworks. Early glass was made in wood-burning furnaces but the discovery of coal at Pittsburg as well as good water transport meant that the town became an important centre. The most famous of these was the Pittsburg Flint Glass Works, established in 1808 by Benjamin Bakewell who made glassware for President Monroe and President Andrew Jackson. The work produced in this factory continued the methods of the preceding century but used the aesthetic conventions of Federal design.

The nineteenth century was, above all, a period of technical innovation. The glass-pressing machine was developed by Demming Jarves (1790–1869). In 1825 John Palmer Bakewell of the Pittsburg Flint Glass Works was the first man to patent pressed glass for the production of furniture-knobs and in 1826 Jarves left the New England Glass Company to establish his own Sandwich Glass Company. Another popular method of manufacturing mass-produced glass in the nineteenth century was blow-moulded glass – many commemorative bottles were produced in this way. To use Jarves' words, 'America can claim credit of great improvements in the needful machinery which has advanced the art to its present perfection'.

From 1864, soda glass developed by William Layton, of the Wheeling Glass Factory of West Virginia, proved to be a very much cheaper substitute for lead glass and this innovation was disastrous for many of the more traditional establishments.

The late nineteenth-century applied and decorative arts are dominated by the name of Tiffany and his 'favrile' glass. Louis Comfort Tiffany was born in 1848, the son of the founder and manager of the successful and famous silversmithing business.

'Louis C. Tiffany and Associated Artists' was established in 1879. One aspect of the firm's activities was designing and making stained-glass windows. Tiffany's interest in stained glass was to extend to the provision of shades for the new electric lights; he set about experimenting with coloured glass and eventually broke the partnership to devote himself to this work. It was Tiffany's wish to emulate the ancient glass he had studied and collected and the measure of his success was well described by Samuel Bing when he wrote: 'If we are called upon to declare the supreme characteristic of this glassware, we would say it resides in the fact that the means employed for the purpose of ornamentation are sought and found in the vitreous substance itself, without the use of either brush, wheel or acid. When

Above: Flask by J. F. Amelung. Dated 1792. (The Corning Museum of Glass, New York.) Below: Marks used by Louis C. Tiffany at the Tiffany Studios

cool, the article is finished'.

'The metallic luster', Tiffany explained, 'is produced by forming a film of a metal or its oxide, or a compound of the metal on or in the glass, either by exposing it to vapors or gasses or by direct application. It may also be produced by corroding the surface of the glass'. The gold lustre, his most popular product, was achieved with gold chloride, either suspended in the glass or sprayed on while the glass was hot from the furnace. After gold the most popular colours were blue, green, white, yellow, brown, amethyst, black and red. Tiffany discovered that glass could be coloured blue with cobalt or copper oxides, green with iron, violet with manganese and red with gold. He further discovered how the use of coke, coal and other carbon oxides resulted in an amber colour, and black could be achieved with a mixture of manganese, cobalt and iron.

In addition to the plain colours and the simple 'Cypriote' ware based on ancient forms, he produced pieces decorated with coloured glass such as his famous peacock-feather ware, agate ware, marbleized glass, flower forms or his simple works decorated with a few trailing ivy-leaves or lily-pads. With Louis Comfort Tiffany, 'Art Nouveau' reached its apogee.

Firearms

The discovery of America by Columbus in 1492 coincided with the development of firearms in Europe. Firearms are thus of greater significance in American history than either armour or edged weapons. In Colonial times most firearms were imported into America and Colonial gunsmiths were for the most part following European models. During The Seven Years' War, Colonial American gunsmiths were encouraged to develop their trade because British troops were out of touch with their supplies.

One of the most famous of all Colonial American firearms is the Kentucky or Pennsylvania rifle with its usually octagonal barrel forty or forty-five inches in length. These guns were derived from the German *Jaeger*, or Hunter's rifle, and apart from their extreme length they are distinguished by the recessed patch-box in the maple or black walnut stock.

After 1820 the flintlock superseded the percussion-cap and many earlier arms were updated by adaptation. The Kentucky long rifle was shortened and generally simplified to become a useful and therefore common firearm on the plains, the opening up of which was heralded by the Louisiana Purchase and the Lewis and Clarke Expedition. The centre of production for the Kentucky rifle was the Appalachian region, whereas the so-called 'plains' rifles were made further west, notably by the Hawken brothers of St. Louis.

America is best known in this field for the production of small hand-guns. The first famous name associated with these is that of Henry Deringer of Philadelphia, who began his career making both rifles and duelling-pistols. Soon after 1825 he began specializing in short pocket-pistols between three and a quarter and nine inches in length with large calibres, .33 to .51 inches. His reputation was such that he inspired many imitations, his name becoming synonymous with a type of pistol which continued to be manufactured many years after his death in 1868.

The Pepperbox, as its name implies, consisted of a

series of barrels grouped around a central axis which could be fired one after another. Manufactured in both Europe and America, it was a step towards the evolution of the revolver.

The revolver may be defined as a gun in which the ammunition revolves automatically in a chambered cylinder for successive discharges through a fixed barrel. Samuel Colt (1814–1862) took out patents in Britain, France and America and by 1836 the American patent was licensed to a succession of manufacturers. To a large extent Colt's success may be associated with his ability to supply arms with interchangeable parts. This was made possible by the emergence of such machine-designers as E. K. Root and F. W. Howe, whose equipment could produce precision work even in unskilled hands. These production methods were applied to Colt's European licensed manufacturers with great success.

Eliphalet Remington Jr. of Ilion, New York, trained as a gunsmith from his earliest youth, making both flint and percussion-cap rifles. By 1849 he had made his first revolver but it remained relatively unknown until he had refined it in 1856. During the Civil War Remington supplied the Government with 128,000 revolvers, not including those made for private customers.

Though repeating and breech-loading guns had been made in the eighteenth century, it was not until the nineteenth century that they were effectively developed and manufactured in large numbers for use in the Civil War and in the west. Smith and Wesson (Horace Smith and Daniel B. Wesson) began developing their repeating pistols and rifles as early as 1831 on the basis of the earlier work of Walter Hunt. Smith and Wesson arms were improved in the mid-nineteenth century by B. Tyler Henry for the famous Henry and Winchester rifles.

John Hall of Yarmouth, Maine, patented one of the most successful breech-loading rifles in 1811. Though his firearms were fairly successful it was Christian Sharps of Philadelphia who later captured the market with his famous rifle. It was Sharps carbines that John Brown used at Harpers Ferry and they remained popular throughout the Civil War with Hiram Berdan and his famous Sharp Shooters.

Textiles

The frontiersman in his leather jerkin and trousers, fringed and decorated in hybrid American/Indian fashion, has long been a figure in American folklore, his attire remaining almost unchanged from the eighteenth century through to the nineteenth. The Quakers of Pennsylvania, with their broad-brimmed hats and sombre clothes, have likewise established their place in the visual history of America.

Though a textile factory was established at Rowley, Massachusetts, as early as 1638, weaving in America remained a cottage industry producing simple textiles such as linsey-woolsey and decorative work woven on a simple, four-harness overshot loom. The double-weave, also known as 'double-face' and 'summer and winter' weave, was less common. Designs include Eight Pointed Star, Lisbon Star, Lovers' Knot, Wheel and Star, Snowball and Wheel of Fortune. Many of these were surrounded by a pine-tree border and are similar to Welsh examples no

doubt due to immigration from the Principality.

In 1814 the power loom was introduced into America by Francis Cabot Lowell after he had visited England and studied the textile industry. American textiles woven on looms using a Jacquard or similar attachment were always the work of professionals. Jacquard, a native of Lyon, invented his loom in 1801 and Jacquard coverlets were being woven in half-width in America by the second quarter of the nineteenth century. The 'fly-shuttle' was invented in England by John Kay of Lancashire as early as 1733, but was not in general use in America until the 1860s and '70s, enabling these coverlets to be woven in full width.

Professional embroiderers were almost unknown in Colonial America; most young ladies were trained to embroider from early childhood. The word 'sampler' or 'examplar' is used to describe those lovingly created or dutifully executed embroideries which were, in the sixteenth and seventeenth centuries, used primarily as a means of recording a repertoire of stitches. Early European samplers consist of a series of fragments of decoration achieved by numerous stitches, whereas late eighteenth- and early nineteenth-century specimens in both Europe and America were conceived as pictorial entities decorated with the alphabet and the numerals one to nine. Most of these early samplers are tall and narrow but during the eighteenth century the proportions generally became more square. Some American specimens are not only signed by the embroideress but, if made in a school, the name of the 'Preceptress' also appears. Among the examples made in America, perhaps the most interesting historically are the genealogical samplers. The Olmstead sampler made in Connecticut in 1774 lists as many as twelve people and gives their dates of birth and marriage. A specifically American character began to appear in samplers of the 1720s and by the early 1800s this trend was firmly established. After about 1830, however, the standard deteriorated.

In the early nineteenth century mourning-pictures were popular. Some were simple water-colours while others were embroidered; occasionally they were a combination of both. All were fairly elaborately framed and glazed with a broad margin of gold-lined black glass.

Bedspreads and bed-hangings embroidered with crewel silks were popular in eighteenth-century America and can be identified by the sparse character of their designs compared with their English equivalents. Crewel-work went out of fashion with the beginning of the Classical Revival.

Printed cottons were popular in America, especially after the Revolution when the designs included subjects such as the Apotheosis of Benjamin Franklin. One of the earliest references to textiles such as these occurs in a letter that Franklin wrote from London to his wife in 1758 telling her what he was sending from England: 'there are also fifty-six yards of cotton printed curiously from copper plates, a new invention to make bed and window curtains; and seven yards of chair bottoms printed in the same way, very neat'. Notwithstanding British mercantile policy, Colonial calico printers were in business, one of the most famous of these being John Hewson of Philadelphia.

That industrialization was deemed to be an important development in early nineteenth-century America may be judged by the fact that Kirk Boot of the Merrimack Manufacturing Company (established at Lowell in 1822) found the firm's manager, John D. Prince, in Manchester. Prince told Boot that he would expect a salary of five thousand dollars per year. 'Why, that is more than we pay the Governor of Massachusetts' exclaimed Boot. 'Can the Governor of Massachusetts print?' Prince sarcastically inquired. He was employed on his own terms. Many other textile factories were operating in nineteenth-century America, especially in New England.

It is usually thought that patchwork was evolved by sewing together a series of otherwise useless pieces of material to form one 'crazy quilt', creating a possession not only of beauty and utility, but also one provided at little extra cost at a time when textiles were extremely valuable.

Pieced patchwork is common to both America and Europe whereas appliqué patchwork was more common in America. Among many examples of geometric pieced patchwork designs the star is a recurrent motif, often alluding to a particular state in the Union. In pre-war days, the 'quilting-bee' was as important socially as the 'sewing-circle' was to become during and after the American Civil War. The perfecting of the design of the sewing-machine in the United States during the third quarter of the nineteenth century also had its effect on the development of this art.

The designs of American patchwork quilts were known by attractive names, although many were interchangeable and some confusion has resulted: the Wandering Foot, Turkey Tracks or Death's Black Darts, Crazy Patchwork, Beggars' Blocks, Robbing Peter to Pay Paul, Star of Bethlehem, Meadow Lily, Tulips, Rose of Sharon, Oak Leaf, Baseballs, Cactus Rose, Tumbling Blocks, Log Cabin, Sunburst, Cake-stand, Lotus Flower, Dresden Plate, Princess Feather and Geometric Snowball. Regional characteristics of design are significant, especially those of the Pennsylvania Germans.

Quilting was a means by which the coverlet top, lining and filling (of carded wool, cotton, or sometimes down) could be held together, though this was also achieved by tying. This utilitarian necessity was customarily used with decorative effect. Elaborate quilting designs were drawn with the help of templates of sized paper or textile. Princess Feather, Star and Crown, Peacock Fan, Oak-leaf, Daisy, Swirl, Acanthus, Day Lily, Starfish, Tea-cup, Running Vine, Pineapple and Spider-web are just some of the many designs used. Simpler quilting designs that did not need templates include Crossbar, Double Crossbar and Diamonds. The finest examples are to be found where quilting forms the only decoration and this 'Italian' or 'Trapunto' quilting is of the very best quality. Quilting was known to pre-Columbian Central American cultures and in ancient China. In Jamestown, Virginia, in the seventeenth century, quilted armour proved to be sufficient protection from stone projectiles.

In seventeenth-century America, floors were either left bare or were covered with rushes, rush mats or animal-skins; carpets, if there were any, were placed upon tables. In the eighteenth century, painted canvas or linen ('American cloth') floor coverings were in use as well as imported Eastern and European carpets. Hooked rugs became popular between 1840 and 1900.

Prints

Between about 1775 and 1830 the aquatint was a popular print-making process that achieved an effect similar to water-colour painting, but the process was soon eclipsed by a new and altogether simpler technique. In 1796 Alois Senefelder invented lithography. Engraving had been treated as an art as early as the seventeenth century by Rembrandt and others but their engravings are, for the most part, independent of their work as painters. Hogarth, who had been trained as a silver engraver, made prints from his own paintings but he was the exception. It was more common for an artist in England to authorize a Bartolozzi, or in America a David Edwin, to produce an authorized version ('sculp') of their paintings ('pinxt'). Following the introduction of lithography it became widespread practice for artists to produce prints after their own paintings. Thus Rembrandt Peale made his own lithographic copy of his portrait of George Washington.

'Falls of Niagara', detail from a map of North America, engraved and published in Philadelphia, 1822

John James Audubon who was born in Haiti in 1785, the natural son of a sea merchant and a Creole chambermaid, has become a household name with his two published works 'Birds of America' and 'The Quadrupeds of America'. Audubon called upon two English engravers, Robert Havell and his son, to reproduce his water-colours. 'Birds of America' was published in four volumes between 1827 and 1838 with a later abridged edition in 1838. In 1844 Audubon, together with John Bachman, began the second definitive work 'The Quadrupeds of America'. Some of the volumes were published before Audubon's death in 1851 and his sons completed the work by 1854. Audubon visited Britain a number of times and in 1826 exhibited his drawings in Edinburgh just as George Catlin (1796–1872) exhibited his paintings of the American Indian in London. However,

Catlin had adopted the new lithographic process to interpret his own work and the 'North American Indian Portfolio' was published in England in 1844.

In the middle of the nineteenth century the age of regular transatlantic travel began and artists such as Edwin Austin Abbey, R.A., who is well known for his murals in Boston Public Library and the State Capital, Harrisburg, Pennsylvania, all but commuted between England and America. He derived his main livelihood from black and white illustrations for 'Harpers' and for various editions of Shakespeare and Dickens.

American print-makers responded enthusiastically to the coming of the railroad. When 'de Wit Clinton', America's first practical steam locomotive appeared on 31 July, 1832, William H. Brown cut a silhouette of the train, and in 1869 Leggo and Company of Montreal made a lithograph from Brown's silhouette. It became the most famous print in this genre and has recurred in several versions.

Mid-nineteenth-century print-making was dominated by Currier and Ives. Bass Otis had first introduced lithography to America in 1819 and by 1824 William and John Pendleton had established the first commercial lithographic studio to which Nathaniel Currier (1813–1888) was apprenticed in 1828.

Currier employed groups of artists, specializing in landscapes and figures, who frequently combined their efforts in making one print which was then hand coloured. Currier's genius lay in his ability to sense the market, to pick on current events at a time when newspapers were seldom illustrated. The firm's repertoire also included sentimental subjects like 'Kittens and Puppies', 'Memory Pieces' and 'Miscellaneous', 'in great variety and all elegant and salable Pictures'. One outlet for these prints was the shop on Nassau Street, New York City. Currier made sure that the pedlars who roamed the country and were moving west with the frontier kept large stocks of his prints and these often depicted the frontier itself. European curiosity about America was fed through a London office. The firm of Currier was established in 1835 to become Currier and Ives in 1862. It closed down in 1907.

In the last years of the nineteenth century, music-covers and illustrated magazines like 'Harpers' usurped a large part of the market that Currier and Ives had developed. It was for such productions that artists such as Winslow Homer and Frederick Remington worked.

During the eighteenth century America relied upon wallpapers imported from England and in the first half of the nineteenth century French woodblock-printed wallpapers predominated. Closely related to these wallpapers are the prints that were used to decorate band-boxes.

Dolls and toys

Among De Bry's engravings based on John White's watercolour drawings is a portrait of an American Indian girl holding a European trade doll in one hand and a rattle in the other. Thus began the long tradition of importing both dolls and toys that declined in the nineteenth century.

Between 1800 and the early 1850s the American population grew from some five million to twenty-three million. The children implicit in these figures needed amusement and that need coincided with early industrialization.

Many early toys were made of wood and thus men trained as woodworkers were among the first to mass-produce toys. William S. Tower of Massachusetts, a carpenter by trade, established the Tower Toy Company, a business that was typical of the enterprising toy-makers of the 1830s.

The first American patent issued to a doll-maker was to Ludwig Greiner (1858) for his papier mâché doll heads. He was followed by others including Izannah Walker (1873) and Mary Steuber (1878). Patents for articulated wooden dolls were taken out by Joel Ellis in 1873, F. D. Martin in 1879 and Henry H. Mason and Luke Taylor in 1881. New materials were on their way and in 1855 Charles and Nelson Goodyear took out a patent for rubber dolls, while in 1881 a patent was granted to M. C. Lefferts and W. B. Carpenter of the Celluloid Manufacturing Company. Ingenuity having developed to a high point in the late nineteenth century, it was inevitable that mechanical dolls would be produced such as those by W. A. Harwood which were patented in 1877, Edison's Phonographic doll and William Webber's singing doll.

The inventiveness of America at this time was particularly apparent in the toys of the Crandalls. Jesse Crandall patented several wood-working machines but is chiefly known for inventing a rocking-horse, mounted on springs that would not damage carpets, and for another form of rocking-horse known as the Shoofly.

One day, Charles Crandall in order to amuse his own children who were convalescing gave them 'off cuts' from the tongued and grooved boxes of his croquet sets. With these, his children built houses, bridges, fences, and other structures, and it was on this basis that Crandall went into business making tongued and grooved building blocks. Crandall's toys were, on occasion, popular with adults and

Left: Clock-work figure on à tricycle, probably made by E. R. Ives. c.1890. (Christie, Manson and Woods Ltd., London).
Above: American eagle from the stern of an American ship. Late nineteenth century. (Arthur and James Ayres Collection)

at one point he was producing per day eight thousand 'Pigs in Clover', a toy consisting of a small box with a glass lid containing a miniature maze through which small ball bearings had to be coaxed to a centre pen.

Metal toys were well in production after the Civil War. Even in pre-Revolution days, tin or, more correctly, tin-plated iron, was a popular material for making anything from candle-sconces to toys. In the 1870s clockwork toys became popular; the best were those produced by the firms of J. and E. Stevens, Althof, Bergman and Company and E. R. Ives. Ives was particularly known for his clockwork trains and in one of his advertisements he claimed to be the first toymaker in the United States to make them.

Folk art

As has been seen in the preceding sections of this introduction, the nineteenth century saw the emergence of a national identity in America. This is particularly true of American folk art. It is true not only of the portraits painted by itinerant artists, but also of the wood-carving of the shipyards, the circus and the fair-ground, of the work that was used to advertise the diverse merchandise available in the main street of a town, or of the whirligig or weather-vane surmounting a village barn. Some of these folk artists were extremely talented. William Rush (1756–1823), a woodcarver of Philadelphia, was a founder member of the Pennsylvania Academy of Fine Arts, the earliest institution of its kind in the United States.

Another famous American folk artist was Edward Hicks (1780–1849) whose work is largely derivative. His 'The Falls of Niagara', painted in 1825, lifts every detail from a vignette in H. S. Tanner's 'Map of North America' of 1822.

This and other examples in no way detract from Hicks' talent, for though the form is identical, he was still able to give his works a unique spirit, the spirit of an agrarian, pre-industrialized America.

Generally, American folk artists of this period, though naïve in outlook, were highly skilled as craftsmen and today most of them are anonymous. We are, nevertheless, by no means uncertain of the quality of their work, be it a patchwork quilt, a ship's figurehead or a carousel animal. Some of the finest specimens of fairground art were carved at Gustav Augustus Dentzels' Carousel factory in Germantown, Pennsylvania, in the 1890s.

Several states in the American Union had a history of colonization by non-British European powers or groups. The popular arts in the south west (Texas, New Mexico, Arizona) show how the Spanish and Indian traditions fused to create objects of devotion for the Adobe Moradas.

The German communities of Pennsylvania continued the traditions that had been established long before in medieval Europe for illuminated birth-certificates and charmingly and flamboyantly painted furniture.

The nineteenth century was a time of great artistic and industrial energy and even the seamen of America produced scrimshaw that is, despite the rigours of whaling, both refined and vigorous.

In England a variety of somewhat ineffectual measures had been taken in an attempt to reduce the number of shop-signs displayed in the high street. In contrast, American shop-signs developed without inhibiting legislation and the cigar-store Indian became, in the late nineteenth century, virtually the symbol of a new and short-lived urban peasantry whose art is admired today in a spirit other than that in which it was created.

DATES		STYLES	MATERIALS	
England	America		England	America
1603–1689	1650–1700	*STUART*	Oak, Elm	Conifers, Oak
1689–1702	1700–1730	*WILLIAM & MARY*	Oak, Walnut, other woods	Cherry, Walnut, red and white Pine
1702–1720	1730–1765	*QUEEN ANNE*	Walnut	American Walnut, Cherry
1720–1759		*EARLY GEORGIAN*	Walnut, Mahogany	Cherry, American Walnut
1759–1765	1765–1800	*CHIPPENDALE* (Rococo)	Mahogany	Cherry, Mahogany, Walnut
1765–1795	1788–1810	*CLASSICAL REVIVAL* (Early Federal in America)	Mahogany, Satinwoods, Painted wood, Compositions	Preceding woods, Maple, Mahogany
1795–1839	1810–1839	*GREEK/EGYPTIAN REVIVAL* (Late Federal in America)	Mahogany, Satinwoods, Painted wood, Brass inlay, Compositions	Mahogany, Maple, Satinwood, Painted wood
1839–1901	1839–1901	*VICTORIAN*	All previous materials and many others; anything from Papier Mâché to Cast Iron.	

American furniture styles can only be vaguely approximated with their English counterparts; from the first the American Colonies produced original designs dependent upon native American woods.

Bibliography

Comstock, Helen, (ed), *The Concise Encyclopedia of American Antiques*, Hawthorn Books Inc., New York 1958

Christensen, E. O., *The Index of American Design*, Macmillan, New York 1959

Nineteenth Century America: Furniture and other Decorative Arts, Exhibition Catalogue published by The Metropolitan Museum of Art, New York 1970

Furniture

Downs, Joseph, *American Furniture*, Macmillan, New York 1952

Montgomery, Charles F., *American Furniture: the Federal Period*, Viking, New York 1966 and Thames and Hudson, London 1967

Nutting, Wallace, *Furniture Treasury*, Macmillan, New York reprinted 1954

Silver

Buhler, Kathyrn C., *American Silver,* World Publishing Company, Cleveland 1950

Ceramics

Barber, Edwin Atlee, *The Pottery and Porcelain of the United States*, G. P. Putnam's Sons, New York third edition 1909

Glass

McKearin, George S., and Helen A., *American Glass,* Crown Publishers, New York 1941

Firearms

Peterson, Harold K., *Arms and Armor in Colonial America, 1526–1783*, The Stackpole Company, Harrisburg, Pennsylvania 1956

Textiles

Little, Frances, *Early American Textiles*, The Century Company, New York 1931

Prints

Comstock, Helen, *American Lithographs*, M. Burrows and Co., Inc., New York 1950

Dolls and Toys

Coleman, Dorothy S., Elizabeth A., Evelyn J., *The Collector's Encyclopedia of Dolls*, Robert Hale and Company, London 1970

McClintock, Marshall and Inez, *Toys in America*, Public Affairs Press, Washington 1959

Folk Art

American Folk Art, Catalogue of the Abby Aldrich Rockefeller Folk Art Collection, Williamsburg, Virginia 1959

1 *Chest of drawers*, probably by Thomas Dennis (1683–1706), Ipswich, Massachusetts. 1678. (Henry Francis du Pont Winterthur Museum, Winterthur, Delaware.) This type of chest of drawers superseded the plain chest; it was often elaborately carved and brightly painted. This particular chest was made for John and Margaret Staniford; it bears their initials and the date 1678 – possibly the year of their marriage. Applied split turnings were a common decorative feature at this time, and the carved strap-work design is also typical.

1

2 *Chest*, Connecticut. 1670–90. (American Museum in Britain, Claverton Manor, Bath.) This chest is of oak and pine, the front three panels carved with a tulip pattern and the middle one centring on the initials WSR.

3 *Keeping-room*, American. Seventeenth century. (American Museum in Britain, Claverton Manor, Bath.) Of typical early Colonial type, this room contains simple turned furniture which is both functional and attractive.

4 *The Perley Parlour*, Boxford, Massachusetts. 1763. (American Museum in Britain, Claverton Manor, Bath.) The panelling in this room is of grained cedar and the pilasters are marbled. The furniture is mainly of the type known as 'American Queen Anne'.

5 *Highboy* by John Pimm (working 1736–53), Boston, Massachusetts. 1740–50. (Henry Francis du Pont Winterthur Museum, Winterthur, Delaware.) Made for Commodore Joshua Loring of Boston, this highboy is made of maple and pine with japanned decorations and a bonnet top. The carved shell shapes and rudimentary cabriole legs are typical of such pieces in the second quarter of the eighteenth century.

6 *Highboy*, Philadelphia. 1765–75. (American Museum in Britain, Claverton Manor, Bath.) The more elaborate cabriole legs, more sophisticated style and the use of mahogany put this bonnet-top highboy at least twenty years further into the eighteenth century than that shown in 5.

7 *Armchair* attributed to John and Hugh Finlay of Baltimore. *c.*1805. (Baltimore Museum of Art, Baltimore.) This chair is one of a large set on which are painted the houses of distinguished citizens of Baltimore; it is thought to be the work of Hugh Finlay who, with his elder brother John, specialized in this type of painted furniture.

8 *Side-chair*, Philadelphia. *c.*1796. (Metropolitan Museum of Art, New York. Gift of Mrs. J. Insley Blair.) This side-chair, one of a set, is painted in several colours in the Hepplewhite manner.

6

9 *Case of drawers* by William Lemon, the carving by Samuel McIntire, Salem, Massachusetts. 1796. (Boston Museum of Fine Arts, Boston. Karolik Collection.) Known as 'the masterpiece of Salem', this magnificent chest-on-chest is in a superb architectural style. Full use is made of the patterned mahogany on the drawer-fronts.

10 *Lady's cabinet and writing-table*, Baltimore. 1795–1810. (Henry Francis du Pont Winterthur Museum, Winterthur, Delaware.) A fine quality example of American cabinet-making, this piece is in mahogany, satinwood and cedar and incorporates an oval mirror and painted and gilt panels.

11 *Armchair*, probably New York. *c.*1870. (Art Institute of Chicago. Suzanne Walter Worthy Fund.) This ornate chair, of gilt and veneered wood and brass, is in the Egyptian revival style, represented by the bird's claw and ball feet, the terminals of the arm-supports in the form of pharaohs' heads and the design of the needlework upholstery.

12 *Commode* by Thomas Seymour (active *c.*1800–42), Boston. 1809. (Boston Museum of Fine Arts, Boston. Karolik Collection.) The top of this commode has a shell pattern painted in the centre of the back and alternating panels of mahogany and satinwood radiate to the outer edge.

13 *Sideboard*, one of a pair by John Aitken, Philadelphia *c* 1797, (Mount Vernon, Virginia. Courtesy of the Mount Vernon Ladies' Association of the Union.) Used by George Washington in his Banqueting Hall at Mount Vernon, this fine piece has the perfection in line and proportion much sought after at that time.

14 *Secretaire* by John Shaw (working in America *c.*1733–1803), Annapolis, Maryland. 1796. (Queen's Room, White House Collection, Washington, D.C.). Born in Scotland, John Shaw set up as a cabinet-maker in Annapolis in 1773. This secretaire, although rather behind the times for the last years of the eighteenth century, is a distinguished piece with crisp outlines and a minute attention to detail.

16

15

15 *Tambour desk* by John and Thomas Seymour, Boston. *c.*1800. (Henry Francis du Pont Winterthur Museum, Winterthur, Delaware.) All the precision and delicacy of the skilled father and son team of the Seymours have gone into the making of this desk. The inlaid work and the mechanism of the sliding tambour doors are particularly fine.

16 *Secretaire*, Connecticut or Rhode Island. 1790–1810. (Henry Francis du Pont Winterthur Museum, Winterthur, Delaware.) This piece, with its fine proportions and such intricate details as the elaborate tracery of the pediment and delicate inlaid work, is a perfect example of the craftsmanship in New England at the turn of the century.

17 *Secretaire*, Baltimore or Philadelphia. *c.*1811. (Metropolitan Museum of Art, New York. Gift of Mrs Russell Sage and others.) Known as the 'Sister's Cylinder Bookcase', this piece is taken from Sheraton's 'The Cabinet Dictionary' of 1803. It is of mahogany and satinwood. A straight drop-front desk is substituted for the cylinder roll-top of Sheraton's design and a graceful pediment echoes the inverted pyramid of the base.

18 *Part of a room containing Shaker furniture*. Early nineteenth century. (American Museum in Britain, Claverton Manor, Bath.) Shaker furniture is the product of a religious sect which decreed austerity and high moral values. Their furniture is simple, clear-cut and worked with fine precision and craftsmanship.

19 *Table or candle-stand*. Connecticut. Late seventeenth century. (American Museum in Britain, Claverton Manor, Bath.) Made of maple and pine and painted red, this small stand with its single turned leg once belonged to Peregrine White, who was born on *The Mayflower* in 1620.

20 *Round stand*, New Lebanon, New York. *c*.1820. (American Museum in Britain, Claverton Manor, Bath.) This stand, made of cherry wood, evolved from early forms of candle-stands. It is typical of the strong, plain, well-made Shaker furniture produced in the first three decades of the nineteenth century.

21

22

21 *Tailoress' counter*, Watervliet, New York. 1820–3: (American Museum in Britain, Claverton Manor, Bath.) Made of pine and curly maple, this piece of Shaker furniture has simple turned drawer-knobs, discreet mouldings along the drawers, tapered legs and a strong, stable construction.

22 *Library table* designed by Frank Lloyd Wright (1867–1959), Chicago. 1908. (Art Institute of Chicago. Gift of Mr and Mrs F. M. Fahrenwald.) The architect Frank Lloyd Wright designed many pieces of furniture closely related to his designs for buildings, and was one of the chief instigators of the fashion for built-in furniture. The clean lines of this table are typical of his work.

23 *The Japanese Parlour* in the William H. Vanderbilt House, New York, decorated by Herter Brothers in the 1880s. The vogue for all things Japanese, which swept the United States in the second half of the nineteenth century, was given full rein in this room. Ceramic art adorns the walls and carved and lacquered furniture fills the room.

24 *Settle* designed by Gustav Stickley (1857–1942), Eastwood, New York. c.1909. (Art Institute of Chicago. Gift of Mr and Mrs John J. Evans.) At the turn of the century American furniture was, in general, over-elaborate and not well made. The designs of craftsmen such as Stickley provided a complete contrast and, when published as 'do-it-yourself' manuals, placed their furniture within reach of a much wider class.

25 *Side-chair* by Lambert Hitchcock (1795–1852), Connecticut. Second quarter of the nineteenth century. (American Museum in Britain, Claverton Manor, Bath.) Lambert Hitchcock established a factory on the Farmington River where men, women and children were employed to produce painted chairs in a variety of styles.

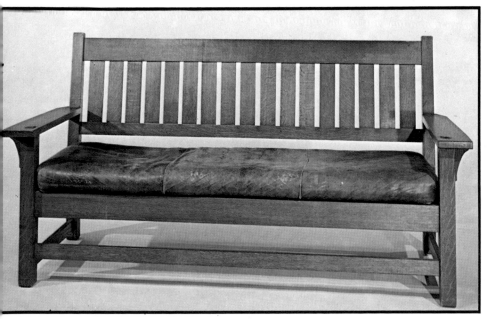

26

27

28

6 *Slipper-chair*, attributed to John Henry Belter (1804–63), New York. Mid-nineteenth century. (American Museum in Britain, Claverton Manor, Bath.) The ree forms of mid-nineteenth-century pieces of this type were made possible by the se of papier mâché or, as in this case, laminated wood. Belter refined this latter nethod by using the steam press to create the basic shapes of his furniture, and in his way achieved some outstanding examples of rococo revival work.

7 *Cabinet-bookcase* designed by Isaac E. Scott (1845–1920), Chicago. Late nineteenth century. (Chicago School of Architecture Foundation. Gift of Mrs harles F. Batchelder.) This piece has close affinities with the work of several con-

temporary English craftsmen. Its Gothic-inspired architectural form and decorative motifs are combined with a frieze of naturalistic birds and vines.

28 *Boston Rocker*, American. Second quarter of the nineteenth century. (American Museum in Britain, Claverton Manor, Bath.) Most such chairs at this time were painted; this one has an unusual stencilled decoration of a locomotive.

29 *Cabinet*, New York. 1875–85. (Private Collection.) This piece is of ebonized wood with inlay, bird's-eye maple and *verre églomisé* panels. It derives from the work of Charles Lock Eastlake, author of 'Hints on Household Taste'.

30 *Square wall-clock* by Chauncey Jerome, American. *c.*1860. (Strike One London.) Made by Chauncey Jerome, one of the most famous firms of American clock-makers, this clock is weight driven and has an eight-day movement. A lower door concealing the weights is fitted into the rosewood case and is decorated by a glass tablet showing the Old State House at Hartford, Connecticut, which was designed by Charles Bulfinch, *c.*1790.

31 *Gothic or beehive clock* by Brewster and Company. *c.*1850. (Strike One London.) Made of heavily stained wood, the stain is possibly disguising a wood of rather inferior quality, suited to a cheap clock designed for the mass market. The door of this clock is decorated with a glass tablet which depicts a boating scene in front of the President's House. Topographical and architectural views were among the most popular subjects for glass paintings.

32 *Girandole clock* by Lemuel Curtis. 1816. (Old Sturbridge Village, Sturbridge, Massachusetts.) The girandole, the most elaborate form of the typical American banjo clock, was developed by Lemuel Curtis of Concord, Massachusetts, and rapidly gained popularity. The girandole acquired its name from the elaborate girandole mirrors of the time, both mirror-frames and clock-cases being decorated with gold leaf. The banjo end of this girandole clock is decorated with an architectural view and the clock itself is surmounted by an eagle with out-spread wings.

30

31

33 *Banjo clock* by Simon Willard, American. *c.*1810. (Old Sturbridge Village, Sturbridge, Massachusetts.) The maker of this clock, Simon Willard, was a farmer's son. His brother, Aaron Willard, specialized in making longcase and shelf-clocks while he himself developed a number of different designs and shapes inspired by the lines of the Montgolfier air-balloons. His most successful clocks, of which the one illustrated is an example, came to be called 'banjo clocks'.

33

34 *Standing salt, candlestick, sugar-caster and tankard* by John Coney (1655–1722), Edward Winslow (1669–1753), and Henry Hurst (*c.*1665–1717), Boston. *c.*1700–10. (Boston Museum of Fine Arts, Boston.) Boston was one of the earliest and most flourishing centres of American silversmithing. Traditions were established there of fine quality craftsmanship and a new and distinctively American style emerged.

35 *Porringers* by John Coney and Peter van Inburgh (1689–1740), Boston. (Yale University Art Gallery, New Haven, Connecticut. M. B. Garvan Collection.) This style of porringer, with flat, pierced handle, was of a characteristic American design.

36 *Beaker and porringer* by Robert Sanderson (1608–93) and John Hull (1624–83), Boston. 1659 and *c.*1655. (Boston Museum of Fine Arts. Loaned by the First Church.) The partnership of Hull and Sanderson, both Englishmen, was formed in 1652 when John Hull was appointed to the task of minting new coinage. Between them they made many pieces, including much ecclesiastical plate.

37 *Teapot* by Jacob Hurd (1702–58), Boston. *c.*1738. (Yale University Art Gallery, New Haven, Connecticut.) Spherical teapots of this type became common early in the eighteenth century and changed very little through the years except for minor features illustrated here by the higher foot, broken spout and elaborate finial.

38 *Two-handled cup and cover,* maker's mark IB, probably for Jurian Blanck, New York. *c.*1695. (Henry Francis du Pont Winterthur Museum, Winterthur, Delaware.) The typically English shape of this piece is embellished with rich Dutch ornament, reminiscent of the styles brought back to England at the Restoration.

39 *Monteith* by John Coney, Boston. Early eighteenth century. (Yale University Art Gallery, New Haven. M. B. Garvan Collection.) The monteith, a bowl used for cooling wineglasses, was rarely made in America; this one is a magnificent example of John Coney's work.

40 *Caudle-cup* by Robert Sanderson, Boston. *c.*1680. (Henry Francis du Pont Winterthur Museum, Winterthur, Delaware.) Cups made in this style, slightly pear-shaped and with two handles, are thought to have contained caudle, a kind of broth given to invalids or convalescents.

40

41

41 *Chocolate pot* by Edward Winslow (1669–1753), Boston. *c.*1720. (Metropolitan Museum of Art, New York. Bequest of A. T. Clearwater.) The first American chocolate pot is recorded in 1690 and is described by its owner as a 'jocolato pot'.

42 *Snuff-box* by Joseph Richardson Sr. (1711–85), Philadelphia. 1750–70. (Yale University Art Gallery, New Haven. M. B. Garvan Collection.) Joseph Richardson was a member of a Quaker family of goldsmiths; he is well known for his many pieces of silverware in the rococo style.

43 *Paul Revere II* by J. S. Copley. 1768–70. (Boston Museum of Fine Arts, Boston. Gift of J. W., W. B. and E. R. Revere.) Paul Revere II (1734–1818), the famous Revolutionary leader, was a competent engraver and prolific silversmith.

44 *Kettle* by Gerardus Boyce, New York. *c.*1840. (S. J. Shrubsole Ltd., London.) This exceptionally rare silver kettle has a swing handle. It is engraved with the crest of the Morgan family.

45 *Sugar box* by Edward Winslow, Boston. *c.*1700. (Henry Francis du Pont Winterthur Museum, Winterthur, Delaware.) The sugar box, like the bowl, was complementary to the caster. Many surviving pieces are American and oval in shape.

46 *Dredger,* maker's mark I.R., probably Joseph Richardson, Philadelphia. *c.*1760. (S. J. Shrubsole Ltd., London.) Dredgers, boxes with perforated lids for sprinkling sugar and other powders, became common in England in the mid-seventeenth century.

47 *Whistle* by Daniel Christian Fueter (active *c.*1754–76), New York. *c.*1760–70. (Yale University Art Gallery, New Haven. M. B. Garvan Collection.) Of chased gold, this whistle is set with bells and has a coral handle.

43

42

44

46

45

47

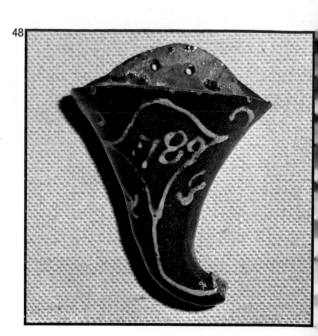

48 *Spill-holder*, American. 1789. (American Museum in Britain, Claverton Manor, Bath.) Made of redware and decorated with yellow slip, this spill-holder would have been nailed to the wall beside a fire. The manufacture of redware, the first pottery to be made in the American Colonies, began in the late 1600s, and continued well into the nineteenth century.

49 *Cup and dish*, American. *c.*1780. (The John Judkyn Memorial, Freshford Manor, Bath.) The redware dish is decorated with slip, creamy liquid clay which was used to decorate a great deal of redware. It was applied by straining it through the holes of a cup, similar to that illustrated on the right. A pure lead glaze was applied over the finished article giving the slip its yellowish colour.

50 *Dish*, American. Late eighteenth century. (American Museum in Britain, Claverton Manor, Bath.) Mottoes, applied in slip, were a popular form of decoration on early slipware.

51 *Bowl*, American. Eighteenth century. (American Museum in Britain, Claverton Manor, Bath.) This redware bowl, decorated with a stylized bird, is covered in a dark brown glaze made mainly of manganese, which was used in varying proportions to make a cheap glaze of tan, brown or black.

52 *Water-carrier*, American. Early nineteenth century. (American Museum in Britain, Claverton Manor, Bath.) Waterbottles were used in particular by farm labourers during the harvest: the men put their arms through the holes and slung them over their shoulders, leaving their hands free to carry tools.

53 *Keg*, American. Nineteenth century. (American Museum in Britain, Claverton Manor, Bath.) Although redware was porous, it could be used for the short-term storage of liquids.

54 *Jug*, American. Nineteenth century. (American Museum in Britain, Claverton Manor, Bath.) This redware jug, coated with cream slip, is decorated with brown and green glazes which have run in the heat of the kiln to produce this attractive, impressionistic effect.

55

55 *Roseville Pottery Company wares,* Zanesville, Ohio. From left to right: *White Rose Vase; Rozane Royal Vase. c.*1905; *Rozane Egypto Candlestick; Rozane Royal vase, c.*1901. (Smithsonian Institution, Washington, D.C.) The Roseville Pottery Company started business in Roseville, Ohio, in 1892, in 1900 acquiring a plant in Zanesville. The initial Roseville line was named 'Rozane' and slip-painted on a dark ground and finished with a high glaze. The name 'Rozane' was usually incised on the ware, frequently accompanied by the letters RPCO (for Roseville Pottery Company). Soon afterwards, Roseville started to bring out new styles with increasing frequency in an effort to match local competition. These tended in the direction of modelled designs in matt-glaze colours.

56 *Weller Dickensware vases,* American. *c.*1902. (Smithsonian Institution, Washington, D.C.) Samuel A. Weller, the owner of a commercial pottery in Zanesville, Ohio, expanded the production of art pottery by adding two or more new styles to his repertoire each year and, in 1910, he advertised his firm as 'the largest pottery in the world . . .' His Dickensware, usually decorated with drawings of characters or scenes from the work of Charles Dickens, was one of his most popular lines.

57 *Van Briggle Pottery Company vases,* Colorado Springs. (Smithsonian Institution, Washington, D.C.) Artus van Briggle, who had been one of the foremost decorators at the Rookwood Pottery until ill health forced him to seek a change in climate, established a pottery at Colorado Springs under his own name in 1901. His belief, that decoration should be an integral part of each shape and not merely an addition to it, is reflected in the flowing form of the Art Nouveau style, characteristic of the work of the Van Briggle Pottery.

58 *Newcomb Pottery vases,* New Orleans. Left: signed by Henrietta Bailey, after 1910. Right: attributed to Marie T. Ryan. 1897–1910. (Smithsonian Institution, Washington, D.C.) The Newcomb Pottery in New Orleans, Louisiana, was organized in 1897 as an adjunct to the art department of the Sophie Newcomb Memorial College for Women. The ware that brought prominence to the southern college pottery was a carved style employing motifs indigenous to its locality – rice, cotton, magnolia and other plants – executed schematically. Miss Sheerer, the director of the Pottery, designed the shapes; the pots were thrown and then decorated by the students. Designs were carved or incised and then delicately sponged, exposing on the body surface a fine sand which served to produce a misty effect beneath the glaze.

56

57

58

59

59 *Rookwood Pottery vase,* American. 1900. (Victoria and Albert Museum, London.) The Rookwood Pottery, the foremost American art pottery, because it was founded by a woman in the days when there were few women *entrepreneurs*, probably received more gratuitous publicity during the first twenty years of its existence than any other American enterprise. Until approximately 1910, Rookwood art pottery was almost entirely confined to pieces individually decorated by the artists who customarily signed their work with their initials or monogram – each piece was also dated, a feature which distinguishes Rookwood from most other art pottery, and given a number which identified the shape.

61

62

60 *Rookwood ceramics,* American. Late nineteenth century. From left to right: *Ewer* with dragon motif, initialled by Albert R. Valentien; *Vase* with portrait of Chief Joseph of the Nez Percés, signed by W. P. McDonald; *Bowl* with Japanese flower motif. (Metropolitan Museum of Art, New York. Gifts of W. M. Sawyer, 1945, and F. J. Kaufman Fund, 1969.) Although floral themes continued to be the most characteristic of the Rookwood Pottery, other decorative shapes appeared in the last decade of the nineteenth century. Among the innovations were under-glaze, slip-painted portraits of American Indians, Negroes, and cats, dogs and other animals. Under the influence of the Art Nouveau movement, several of the artists attempted to interest the Pottery in making sculptured art forms, but this style apparently proved unpopular in the salerooms and was not encouraged by the management.

61 *Vase,* Tucker Factory, Philadelphia. *c.*1830. (American Museum in Britain, Claverton Manor, Bath.) Started in about 1825 by William Ellis Tucker, the Tucker factory produced the first fine American porcelain. The factory continued under various names, chiefly Tucker and Hemphill, until 1838. The style of decoration on the white, hard-paste wares was much influenced by French designs, as seen on this neo-classical urn which owes its inspiration to Sèvres products of this period.

62 *Jug,* Tucker Factory, Philadelphia. 1828. (American Museum in Britain, Claverton Manor, Bath.) Painted with polychrome flowers and gilt, the initials 'ES' under the spout of this jug are believed to stand for the original owner, Elizabeth Slater. After the break-through by Tucker, American porcelain manufacturers began to establish themselves and by 1875 the United States had a true porcelain industry.

63

63 *Jug*, Tucker Factory, Philadelphia. *c.*1830. (Smithsonian Institution, Washington, D.C.) Like all Tucker ware, this jug is made of French-type hard paste porcelain and the floral decoration shows a strong French influence.

64 *Cup and saucer*, Tucker Factory, Philadelphia. *c.*1830. (The John Judkyn Memorial, Freshford Manor, Bath.) Made during the Tucker-Hulme partnership, this cup and saucer are part of a service made for the Hulme family. The cup is twelve-faceted and decorated with a stylized vine motif while the saucer is sixteen-faceted, picked out in gilt, and bears an incised mark on the base.

65 *Mug and bowl*, Chinese export. *c.*1800. (Smithsonian Institution, Washington, D.C.) Blue and white Chinese export wares comprised the main body of porcelain used in Colonial America and continued to be in use after the Revolution. Although they were generally inferior to pre-Revolutionary imports, of particular interest are services made or decorated specially to order in Canton, as is the case with this mug painted in polychrome with the Great Seal of the United States and the borders decorated with the Nankin pattern.

64

67

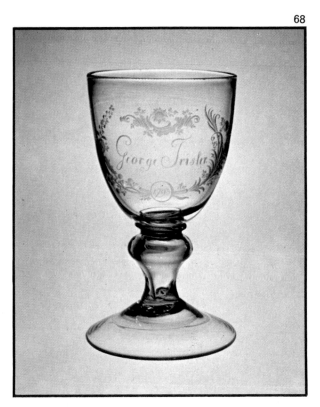

68

66 Left: *Covered sugar-bowl,* German. *c.*1780. Centre and right: *Covered sugar-bowl and candlestick,* attributed to a South Jersey glassworks, possibly Wistar's. *c.*1760–80. (Corning Museum of Glass, Corning, New York.) The most noteworthy and best known of the American glasshouses in the eighteenth century were those established by Caspar Wistar, Henry William Stiegel and, later, John Frederick Amelung. Wistar, formerly a successful brass button manufacturer in Philadelphia, established his glass factory just south east of Philadelphia in 1769 and imported many of his glass-workers from Germany and Holland. The covered sugar-bowl made of colourless glass on the left, with its chicken finial, represents a prototype on which many American pieces were later to be based. Pieces from Wistar's factory and later South Jersey glasshouses are referred to today as 'South Jersey Type' glass and the general style which gradually spread to window- and bottle-glasshouses in New England and New York State is called the 'South Jersey Tradition'.

67 *Covered tumbler* by John F. Amelung, New Bremen. 1788. (Corning Museum of Glass, Corning, New York.) John Frederick Amelung, a practical glassmaker from Grünenplan, Germany, was an outstanding figure in eighteenth-century glassmaking in America. He established a small community at New Bremen in Maryland where, by 1785, he was offering 'window glass, and green and white hollow wares to the public'. Among the earliest pieces of glass known to have been made by Amelung is this covered tumbler which is engraved with a vignette of Tobias and the Angel. It was made by Amelung as an anniversary gift to his wife in 1788 and bears the inscription 'Happy is he who is blessed with virtuous children. Carolina Lucia Amelung. 1788'.

68 *Pokal* (goblet), one of a pair by John F. Amelung, New Bremen. 1793. (Corning Museum of Glass, Corning, New York.) This large goblet, with its high, domed foot and baluster stem made with a pair as presentation pieces for Amelung's friend, George Trisler, represents a style which had been fashionable some fifty years earlier in Germany. As in all the decorative arts, there was a time-lag in the adaptation of American styles in glass from European precedent.

69

70

71

69 *Enamelled tumblers* by Henry W. Stiegel, Manheim. 1772–74. (Corning Museum of Glass, Corning, New York.) Stiegel began producing enamelled glass in 1772, undoubtedly to supply the local Pennsylvania German market.

70 *Flask* by John F. Amelung, New Bremen. 1792. (Corning Museum of Glass, Corning, New York.) Engraved 'F. Stenger. 1792', it is made of free-blown, smoky, green-tinted glass.

71 Left to right: *Diamond pattern-moulded pocket bottle; Chequered diamond pattern-moulded pocket-bottle; Blue glass salt;* Engraved goblet; American, the latter three pieces attributed to the New Bremen Glass Manufactory. Late eighteenth century. (New Orleans Museum of Art, New Orleans, Louisiana.)

72 *Pitcher,* South Jersey type, possibly Lancaster or Lockport glassworks, New York. c.1840–50. (Corning Museum of Glass, Corning, New York.) This pitcher in the so-called 'South Jersey style' is made of free-blown glass and decorated with the lily-pad motif.

73 *Covered goblet and pitcher,* attributed to the Boston and Sandwich Glass Company, Sandwich, Massachusetts. 1870–88. (Sandwich Glass Museum.) Made by a factory first noted for its 'lacy' pressed glass, these pieces are of clear glass with mechanically threaded decoration.

74 *Plated Amberina vase,* New England Glass Company. c.1880. (Corning Museum of Glass, Corning, New York. Mr. and Mrs. Richard Greger Collection.) A patent was issued for the New England Glass Company's plated Amberina in 1886. Made of Amberina encasing an opaque-white glass, it is almost always pattern-moulded.

74

73

75 *Wisteria lamp,* Tiffany Studios. *c.*1900. (Sotheby's Belgravia, London.) In the true Art Nouveau tradition, this lamp is made to resemble wisteria rather than just decorated with motifs derived from wisteria: the form of lamps and vases took on that of objects in nature and thus a flower vase might be a vase resembling the shape and colour of a flower. The lamp is made of leaded marble glass outlined, like a stained glass window, in verdigris bronze, with a base of the same material.

76 *Royal Flemish bottle,* Mount Washington Glass Company. *c.*1890. (Corning Museum of Glass, Corning, New York. L. K. Ford Collection.) The firm has been called the 'Headquarters in America for Art Glass'. Often exotic in form and decoration, Royal Flemish is a colourless glass decorated with thin stains and raised gilding.

77 *Amberina bottle,* New England Glass Company. 1883–88. (Corning Museum of Glass, Corning, New York.) Amberina was the first bi-partite, or shaded, glass to achieve popular approval: it was patented in 1883 by Joseph Locke, an emigré Englishman. The colour gradually changes from amber near the base to a deep ruby red at the top. This fine example of American art glass is pattern moulded.

76

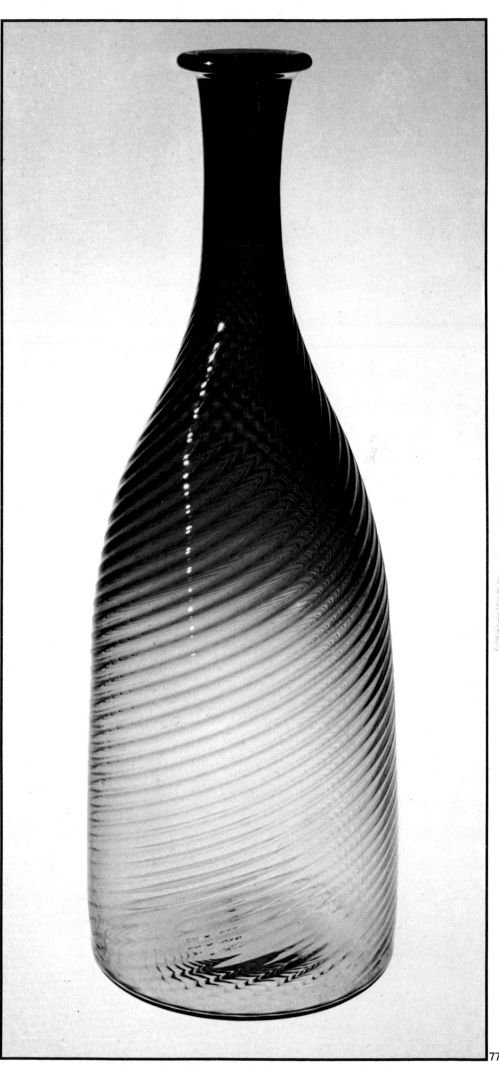

77

78

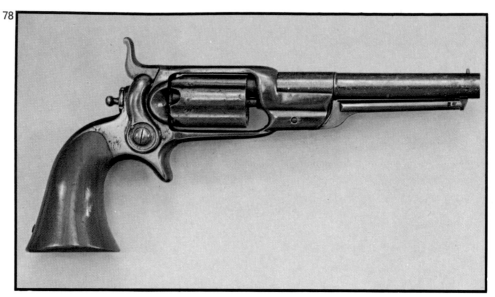

79

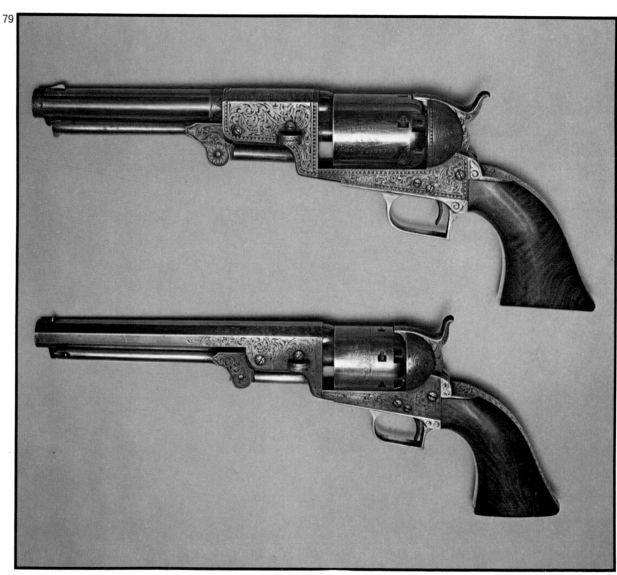

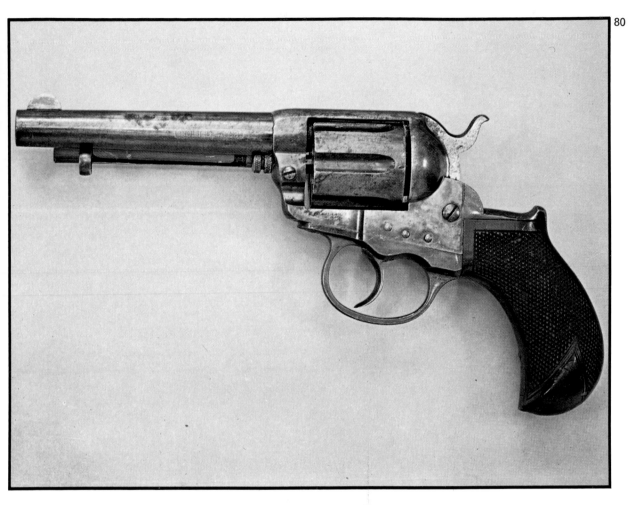

80

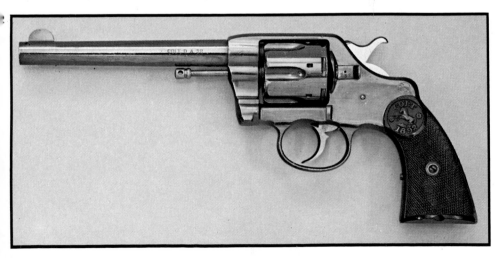

78 *Colt percussion revolver,* the design credited to Elisha K. Root, introduced in 1857. (H.M. Tower of London Armouries.) Elisha K. Root was the Superintendent and later the President of the factory set up by Samuel Colt in Connecticut in the middle of the nineteenth century. This revolver is a five-shot, single-action, .265 calibre, barrel length 4½ inches.

79 Above: *Dragoon percussion revolver,* Colt model. 1848. (By gracious permission of H.M. The Queen.) This weapon is presentation engraved, six-shot, single-action, serial number 9628, .44 calibre, barrel length 7½ inches, unloaded weight 4 lbs. Below: *Navy percussion revolver,* Colt model. 1851. (By gracious permission of H.M. The Queen.) Presentation-engraved, six-shot, single action, .36 calibre, barrel length 7½ inches; this revolver is similar to the one above and belongs to the same group.

80 *Colt Lightning revolver.* (H.M. Tower of London Armouries.) Six-shot, breech-loading, .38 centre-fire calibre, barrel length 4½ inches. This revolver which has a rod ejector, is one of the two double-action, solid-framed models introduced into the Colt range in 1878.

81 *Peace-maker Colt Model 1873 revolver.* (H.M. Tower of London Armouries.) Six-shot, single-action, breech-loading, barrel length 7½ inches. This revolver has a rod ejector and ivory grips to the butt. This type was undoubtedly the best-known Colt revolver, by virtue of its association with the American West. It was also known as the 'Frontier Six-Shooter' or the 'Single-Action Army'. This model in twenty different calibres and five barrel lengths, was made from 1873 to 1940 and production was resumed in 1957.

82 *New Double-Action Army revolver,* Colt Model 1892. (H.M. Tower of London Armouries.) Six-shot, double-action, .38 centre-fire calibre, barrel length 6 inches. These weapons had the swing-out cylinder introduced by the Colt company in 1889, and were the first of such arms to be issued to the United States Army.

83

84

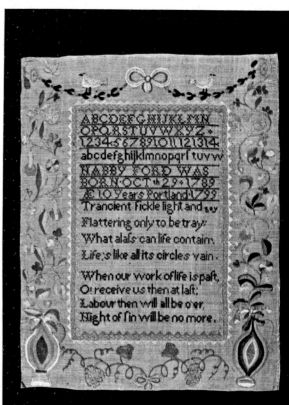
85

83 *Sampler* by Elizabeth Lawson. 1833. (The John Judkyn Memorial, Freshford Manor, Bath.) Samplers were made in America from the seventeenth century. Many later ones were of this type, with the alphabet, numerals and a genealogical table worked in cross-stitch and surrounded by a floral border.

84 *Sampler* by Charlotte Glubb, Washington City. 1813. (American Museum in Britain, Claverton Manor, Bath.) Pictorial samplers such as this were highly decorative. Verses or proverbs were often worked into the sampler and an angular, geometric border pattern did not detract the eye too much from the main picture.

85 *Sampler* by Nabby Ford, Portland, New Hampshire. 1799. (American Museum in Britain, Claverton Manor, Bath.) Pious verses were thought suitable subjects to employ the little girls who were put to work on samplers. Nabby Ford, who worked this one at the age of ten, probably gained far more pleasure from sewing the colourful and highly decorative border.

86 *Quilted patchwork coverlet,* Baltimore. *c.*1850. (American Museum in Britain, Claverton Manor, Bath.) Quilting was a decorative and effective method of evenly distributing and keeping in place the filling of a coverlet. Many elaborate designs and stitches were used, and patchwork or appliqué work was often used. This coverlet is of printed calico with a diamond-quilted background.

87 *The Quilting Party,* American. *c.*1858. (Abby Aldrich Rockefeller Folk Art Collection, Williamsburg, Virginia.) A painting showing quilting as a central feature of American domestic life. The ladies are seated round a table, working on a red and black squared quilt, their scissors and other implements around them; their menfolk drink and talk.

88 *Stencilled coverlet,* Connecticut. *c.*1830. (American Museum in Britain, Claverton Manor, Bath.) This room is from the Joshua La Salle house, Windham. The stencilled decoration was probably executed by a travelling artist in exchange for board and lodging and a small wage.

92

93

Audubon prints. The coloured engravings reproduced on these pages are the work of John Audubon (1785–1851), who is considered to be perhaps the finest naturalist painter in history. It was his ambition to produce a publication of life-size, full-colour paintings of every known species of American bird, in its natural surroundings and with a written description. After many years of set-backs and financial difficulties, but constant determination to finish his work, the series 'Birds of America' appeared from 1827 to 1838. The next task Audubon set himself was the production of 'The Quadrupeds of North America' with John Bachman. He died in 1851, before the work was completed. Audubon's work is distinguished for its vigour, colour and detailed observations of the wild life he loved.

89 *White-crowned Pigeon* (Columba leucocephala).

90 *Meadow Lark* (Sturnus ludovicianus).

91 *Common American Wildcat* (Lynx rufus).

92 *Virginian Partridge* (Perdix Virginiana).

93 *Carolina Parrot* (Psittacus carolinensis).

Currier and Ives prints. The prints on these pages are coloured lithographs by the firm of Currier and Ives. Nathaniel Currier (1813–88), a printer and publisher in New York, took James Merritt Ives (1824–95) into his firm in 1852; Ives gradually moved up in the firm and Currier took him into partnership with him in 1865. In the days before illustrated daily newspapers, the firm did a good business in prints of current events and personalities of the day, and they also listed among their subjects 'Juvenile, Domestic, Love Scenes, Kittens and Puppies, Ladies Heads, Catholic Religious, Patriotic, Landscapes, Vessels, Comic, School Rewards and Drawing Studies, Flowers and Fruits, Motto Cards, Horses, Family Registers, Memory Pieces and Miscellaneous in great variety, and all elegant and saleable Pictures'.

94

95

96

97

99

94 *Midnight race on the Mississippi.* 1875. (American Museum in Britain, Claverton Manor, Bath.)
95 *Loading cotton on the Mississippi.* 1870. (American Museum in Britain, Claverton Manor, Bath.)
96 *New York Ferry Boat.* Second half of the nineteenth century. (American Museum in Britain, Claverton Manor, Bath.)
97 *Crossing the Rockies.* Second half of the nineteenth century. (American Museum in Britain, Claverton Manor, Bath.)
98 *The Bay of Annapolis, Nova Scotia.* c.1880. (Private Collection.)
99 *The Independent Gold Hunter on his way to California,* by N. Currier. c.1845. (American Museum in Britain, Claverton Manor, Bath.)

98

100 *Bandbox. c.*1830. (American Museum in Britain, Claverton Manor, Bath.) A bandbox is a cylindrical box of pasteboard or thin wood designed to contain light articles of attire, such as hats and gloves, and other personal effects; they were used for purposes of storage and transportation and must have made a pretty sight on a dressing-room shelf or a station platform. The ones illustrated here are all made of wood rather than pasteboard.

101 *Bandbox. c.*1830. (American Museum in Britain, Claverton Manor, Bath.) The nineteenth century was the great period of bandboxes in the United States and they were especially popular in the 1830s.

102 *Bandbox. c.*1840. (American Museum in Britain, Claverton Manor, Bath.) The papers decorating these bandboxes are block printed. With this one the decoration suggests the influence of the Orient.

103 *Bandbox. c.*1830. (American Museum in Britain, Claverton Manor, Bath.) The decorations on bandboxes often depict topical and historic events and well-known views; here, the Merchant's Exchange in New York is shown.

104 *Bandbox. c.*1830. (American Museum in Britain, Claverton Manor, Bath.) Volunteer fire-brigades were an important feature of city life; pictured here are lay firemen at work with their equipment.

105 *Bandbox. c.*1850. (American Museum in Britain, Claverton Manor, Bath.) Jenny Lind, the 'Swedish Nightingale', sang at Castle Garden, shown here, when she toured the United States between 1850 and 1852.

106 *Bandbox. c.*1830. (American Museum in Britain, Claverton Manor, Bath.) Similar boxes were in use in Europe for hats, but they were seldom so delightfully coloured and patterned as their American counterparts.

101

104

102

105

103

106

107

107 *Eagle*, from the stern of an American ship. Nineteenth century. (Private Collection.) Ship-carvings – figureheads, sternboards and other embellishments – often produced in the shipyards, are an important aspect of folk art in the United States. This majestic crouching bird has, however, hardly a trace of the naive quality that is often apparent in folk art.

108 *Weathervane. c.*1820. (American Museum in Britain, Claverton Manor, Bath.) This is in the form of an American Indian and stands about three feet high. The colour, worn by exposure to the elements, was brought about by the application of gold leaf to the metal.

108

109

110

111

109 *Birth certificate.* 1844. (American Museum in Britain, Claverton Manor, Bath.) Birth, baptismal and marriage certificates were often beautifully produced in the German communities of Pennsylvania. They were mainly the work of itinerant scribes, or of resident schoolmasters with a good hand, and they are a kind of survival of the medieval illuminated manuscript.

110 *Theorem painting.* Nineteenth century. (American Museum in Britain, Claverton Manor, Bath.) A theorem painting is a stencil painting on velvet. Furniture sometimes had a stencilled decoration of this kind.

111 *Carousel figure of a giraffe.* Nineteenth century. (American Museum in Britain, Claverton Manor, Bath.) Early circus roundabouts were furnished with beautifully carved wooden birds and beasts, both real and imaginary. Carved figures also appeared on the showpieces that announced the arrival of a fair or circus.

112

112 *Kewpie doll. c.*1920. (Kay Desmonde Antiques, London.)
In the style designed by Ernesto Peruggi and copyrighted by
the Manhattan Toy and Doll Manufacturing Company, this
doll is made of rubber. Kewpie dolls were popular in the early
years of the century; they were made of many different
materials and often dressed in costumes such as those of
soldiers, farmers, cowboys or musicians.

113 *Stockinet fabric doll* by Martha Chase, Pawtucket,
Rhode Island. *c.*1910. (Kay Desmonde Antiques, London.)
Dolls of this type were made by stretching the stockinet fabric
over a mask with raised features; the bodies were of pink
sateen or heavy cotton, stuffed. The face was coated with size
and painted with oil colours.

113